PANDA

Dylanna Press

Giant pandas are **mammals** that are native to the bamboo-filled mountains of central China. While they once roamed across much of eastern and southern China, today they can only be found in six isolated mountain ranges in Sichuan, Shaanxi, and Gansu provinces.

These bears are known for their striking black and white fur, with black patches around their eyes, ears, and limbs that stand out against their white bodies. Their scientific name is *Ailuropoda melanoleuca*, which means "black and white cat-foot," referring to their unique coloring and the way they walk.

Despite their cuddly appearance, giant pandas are true bears and belong to the family Ursidae, making them distant cousins to other bear species like the American black bear and brown bear. They are sometimes called "bamboo bears" because bamboo is almost all they eat, making their diet one of the most specialized of any bear species in the world.

---

mammals – warm-blooded animals characterized by having hair or fur, giving birth to live offspring, and typically producing milk to feed their young

Pandas are among the most distinctive-looking animals in the world, instantly recognizable with their black and white pattern that's as unique as a fingerprint. Don't let their round, furry appearance fool you, pandas are surprisingly large and strong bears. An adult panda standing on all fours is about as tall as a kitchen counter (2 to 3 feet [60 to 90 cm]) and 4 to 6 feet (120 to 180 cm) in length. Female pandas typically weigh between 155 to 220 pounds (70 to 100 kg), while males are larger, weighing 190 to 275 pounds (86 to 125 kg).

Panda bears have round heads with characteristic black patches around their eyes, creating their famous "mask." Their ears are also black and rounded, standing out against their white face. They have a relatively short, stubby tail measuring only about 4 to 6 inches (10 to 15 cm) long. Their thick white fur is decorated with black patches on their legs, shoulders, chest, and ears, creating a pattern that serves two important purposes. In their snowy mountain **habitat**, this coloring helps **camouflage** them, while also helping them stand out to other pandas during mating season.

Perhaps their most remarkable feature is what scientists call their "false thumb"—an enlarged wrist bone that works like a thumb. This allows them to grasp and manipulate bamboo with remarkable **dexterity**, similar to how humans use chopsticks. This special adaptation is so unique that no other meat-eating mammal has anything quite like it.

---

habitat – natural environment where an animal lives

camouflage – special coloring or patterns that help an animal blend in with its surroundings

dexterity – skill in using your hands (or in a panda's case, their paws and false thumb) to handle things precisely

Pandas are among the most specialized eaters in the animal kingdom, with bamboo making up an astounding 99 percent of their diet. Unlike most bears, which are **omnivorous**, pandas have evolved to depend almost entirely on bamboo for their survival.

An adult panda spends 10 to 16 hours a day eating, consuming 20 to 40 pounds (9 to 18 kg) of bamboo daily to meet their nutritional needs. This large intake is necessary because bamboo is very low in nutrients—pandas can only digest about 17 percent of what they eat. To maximize their nutrition, pandas are selective about which parts of the bamboo plant they eat. They prefer tender shoots and leaves, switching between species of bamboo and plant parts depending on the season. In spring, they feast on protein-rich shoots, while in fall and winter they rely more on leaves.

Pandas have evolved to reflect their specialized bamboo diet. Their skulls are uniquely shaped with extra-large molars and powerful jaw muscles that can crush tough bamboo stalks. Unlike other bears, pandas' teeth are broader with deeper ridges that help them grind **fibrous** plant material. Their digestive systems are also uniquely adapted to bamboo—they have thick-walled stomachs to protect against splinters and unique gut bacteria that help break down tough plants.

While bamboo is their primary food source, pandas will occasionally eat other plants growing in their habitat, including grasses and wild tubers. In captivity, they enjoy treats like apples and sweet potatoes. Modern pandas have lost most of their ability to digest meat, though they may occasionally eat small rodents.

Water is also crucial for pandas, and they typically drink fresh water daily from streams and rivers in their mountain habitat. They prefer to live near running water sources, which is one reason why protecting mountain watersheds is so important for panda conservation.

---

omnivores – animals that eat both plants and meat

fibrous – something that contains lots of tough, stringy material that is hard to break down and digest

Pandas have developed remarkable physical **adaptations** that make them perfectly suited to their bamboo forest habitat.

- **Powerful Jaws:** Pandas have incredibly strong jaw muscles and broad, flat molars specially designed for crushing tough bamboo. Their jaw strength is among the strongest of all carnivores, allowing them to process up to 40 pounds (18 kg) of bamboo per day.

- **Pseudo-thumb:** One of their most unique adaptations is their "false thumb"—an enlarged wrist bone that acts like an opposable thumb. This special feature allows them to handle bamboo stems with amazing precision, skillfully stripping leaves and shoots.

- **Distinctive Skull:** Their skulls and teeth have evolved to withstand the crushing force needed to process bamboo. Their wider molars and robust jaw muscles contribute to their characteristic round-faced appearance.

- **Low Metabolism:** Pandas have a lower metabolism compared to other bears, which aligns with their low-energy diet of bamboo. This slower rate of burning energy is a critical adaptation that allows them to thrive on a diet that is relatively low in nutrients.

- **Thick Fur:** Their dense, woolly coat keeps them warm in their cool mountain habitat and may provide camouflage in their environment of snow, rocks, and deep forest shadows.

- **Enhanced Forelimbs:** Pandas have strong, muscular front limbs and broad, flat feet with furry soles that aid in gripping bamboo and maintaining balance on steep, slippery terrain.

- **Keen Sense of Smell:** While their eyesight and hearing are only moderate, pandas have a highly developed sense of smell that helps them locate the most nutritious bamboo plants and identify other pandas during mating season.

These specialized adaptations make pandas uniquely suited to their bamboo-eating lifestyle in the mountains of central China.

---

adaptations – ways in which a species becomes fitted into its natural environment to increase its chance of survival

Pandas have developed several fascinating ways of moving and using their bodies that make them unique among bears. While most bears walk with a straight-legged gait, pandas have developed a distinctive side-to-side waddle that comes from their specialized body structure. This rolling walk might look awkward, but it's perfectly suited to their lifestyle and the terrain of their bamboo forest habitat.

Pandas are masters of energy conservation, which is essential given their low-nutrient bamboo diet. When feeding, they adopt a unique sitting posture that helps them conserve energy. They can sit upright for hours, using their strong hind legs to maintain balance while their front paws remain free to handle bamboo. They often feed in a relaxed position, leaning against a tree or rock to support their weight.

Despite their roly-poly appearance and relaxed feeding style, pandas can be surprisingly athletic when they need to be. They're capable climbers, though they spend less time in trees than most other bear species. When motivated—especially if startled or during play—pandas can move quickly over short distances.

Pandas are also excellent swimmers. They're confident in water and often enjoy playing in streams and pools on hot days. Their broad paws and buoyant fur help them swim effectively, and they've been known to cross rivers to reach new feeding grounds or during mating season. In their mountain habitat, this ability to swim helps them navigate the landscape of streams and rivers that cut through their territory.

Pandas are solitary by nature, spending most of their lives alone and generally avoiding direct contact with other pandas. However, these bears have fascinating ways of communicating with each other from a distance, using their excellent sense of smell and a variety of sounds to share messages with other pandas.

During breeding season, which occurs in spring between March and May, pandas become more social and communicative. Males will seek out females by following their scent and distinctive **vocalizations**. Pandas have a diverse range of calls, including chirps, honks, barks, and growls. They use different sounds to express various emotions and intentions—from warnings to gentle communications between mothers and cubs.

While adult pandas prefer solitude, the bond between a mother and her cub is incredibly strong. Cubs stay with their mothers for 18 to 24 months, learning essential survival skills like how to select the best bamboo and climb trees safely. During this time, mothers are extremely protective and attentive, watching over their cubs constantly and sheltering them from danger.

Young pandas engage in playful behavior that helps them develop important physical and social skills. They can often be seen tumbling, wrestling, and climbing under their mother's watchful eye. This play behavior helps strengthen their muscles and improve the coordination they'll need as adults.

Despite their generally solitary nature, research has shown that pandas are more social than previously thought. Trail cameras have captured multiple pandas feeding in the same bamboo grove at different times, suggesting they may have a complex social network based on mutual tolerance and indirect communication through scent marking.

---

solitary – living alone, not in groups

vocalizations – the sounds an animal makes

Pandas maintain well-defined **territories** in their mountain forest homes. Adult pandas typically occupy a range of 1.5 to 3 square miles (4 to 8 square kilometers), though the size can vary depending on the quality and abundance of bamboo in the area. Female pandas often have smaller, more concentrated territories in areas with the best bamboo resources, while males may range more widely, especially during breeding season.

Like many bears, pandas have an excellent sense of smell and use scent marking to communicate with other pandas. They have special glands near their tails that produce a waxy substance which they rub on trees to mark their territory. They also communicate through scratch marks on trees and by leaving droppings in prominent places. These markers help pandas avoid confrontations and allow males to find females during mating season.

Pandas don't migrate long distances, but they do move up and down the mountains throughout the year, following the growth patterns of different bamboo species. When one type of bamboo finishes producing shoots or begins to flower and die, pandas will shift to areas where other species are more plentiful. This is one reason why protecting large, connected areas of habitat is crucial for panda survival.

Unlike many bears that hibernate, pandas remain active year-round because their bamboo food source is available in all seasons. However, they do seek out sheltered places to rest and sleep, often using natural caves, hollow trees, or dense thickets of vegetation. Female pandas become particularly careful about choosing den sites when preparing to give birth, selecting secure, dry caves or tree hollows where they can protect their tiny, vulnerable newborn cubs.

---

territories – areas that an animal claims as its own and defends from others of the same species

Unlike most bears that are active mainly at dawn and dusk, pandas have a unique daily schedule that revolves around their demanding bamboo diet. They don't follow strict day or night patterns—instead, their day is broken into many shorter cycles of eating and resting, repeating about six times throughout each 24-hour period.

A typical panda needs to eat 20-40 pounds of bamboo each day. They usually feed for 2-4 hours at a time, followed by short "food comas"—rest periods that help them digest all that bamboo. During these breaks, they might doze for an hour or two, often finding a comfortable spot propped against a rock or tree. Even while resting, pandas stay alert to their surroundings, using their keen sense of smell to detect anything unusual.

Pandas are most active when temperatures are mild, particularly during the cooler morning and evening hours in summer. On hot days, they might seek out shady areas or even take a refreshing dip in a stream. During heavy rain or snow, they often shelter in hollow trees or caves, though they still need to venture out regularly to eat.

Between eating and resting, pandas spend time grooming their thick fur, which helps keep them clean and comfortable in their humid mountain environment.

This carefully balanced daily routine—eating, resting, and grooming—allows pandas to thrive on their uniquely challenging bamboo diet while conserving the energy they need to survive in their mountain forest home.

Giant pandas have a unique and complex reproductive system that has made them one of nature's most challenging species to breed. Female pandas are fertile for only 24-36 hours once per year, typically between March and May, making successful reproduction a rare and precious event in the wild.

During breeding season, male pandas become more active and vocal, using their keen sense of smell to track females. They may travel long distances to find a mate. Males sometimes compete for females through vocalizations and occasionally physical confrontations, though serious fights are rare.

After mating, something amazing happens. The mother panda's body can actually pause the development of the tiny embryo until conditions are just right for having a baby. Scientists call this "delayed implantation," and it helps ensure cubs are born when bamboo is most nutritious. The total pregnancy lasts between 95 to 160 days.

Pandas usually give birth to a single cub, though twins occasionally occur. When a cub is born, it's one of the smallest newborn mammals in the world compared to its mother's size. A newborn cub weighs only about 3 to 5 ounces (85-140 grams)—about as much as an apple—while its mother weighs hundreds of pounds! This size difference is so extreme that if human babies were born at the same proportion to their mothers, they would be the size of a mouse.

Newborn pandas are one of nature's most helpless babies. They're born pink, hairless, and so tiny that the mother can hold her cub in one paw. Cubs can't even open their eyes for the first 6-8 weeks of life. Mother pandas show amazing dedication to their cubs, holding them close to keep them warm and protected, rarely leaving the den even to eat or drink during those early weeks.

For the first year of life, cubs drink only their mother's milk. Around 6 months old, they begin to taste bamboo and play with it, but they won't be ready to eat it as their main food until they're about 18 months old. During this time, the mother panda teaches her cub everything it needs to know about surviving in the wild—from climbing trees safely to choosing the best bamboo to eat.

Young pandas stay with their mothers longer than many other animals—usually until they're 18-24 months old. This long time together ensures cubs learn all the survival skills they'll need. Once they're ready, young pandas leave their mothers to find their own territory and begin their independent lives in the mountain forests.

Unlike many animal families, father pandas don't help raise the cubs. Mother pandas do all the parenting on their own, and they're so devoted to their cubs that they usually only have one cub every two years. This means female pandas typically only breed every other year in the wild, which is one reason why pandas reproduce more slowly than many other animals.

Pandas play a vital role in their mountain forest home, helping to keep their **ecosystem** healthy in surprising ways. Scientists call pandas an "umbrella species" because protecting pandas also protects countless other plants and animals that share their habitat—just like an umbrella shields everything underneath it.

As bamboo-eating specialists, pandas help maintain their forest's health and diversity. Each day, an adult panda eats 20-40 pounds of bamboo. By eating so much bamboo, pandas help prevent it from taking over the forest floor, allowing other plants to grow. When pandas break and crush bamboo stalks while eating, they create spaces where new bamboo shoots can sprout.

As pandas move through their habitat, they create natural paths through the thick bamboo. These trails become like forest highways for many other amazing animals, including golden snub-nosed monkeys with their bright blue faces, rare blood pheasants with their rainbow feathers, and even the mysterious snow leopard. When we protect panda habitat, we're also protecting homes for hundreds of other species, from tiny leaf deer no bigger than a house cat to giant salamanders as long as a person is tall!

Even panda droppings help the forest! Each day, a panda produces as much droppings as it eats (20-40 pounds). These droppings contain special bacteria that help break down bamboo and other plants, enriching the soil like natural fertilizer.

Also important, by protecting the bamboo forests where pandas live, we also protect the mountains that provide clean water for millions of people. These forests help prevent soil from washing away during rains and keep rivers flowing clean and clear. This makes pandas not just beautiful animals, but important guardians of their mountain home.

---

ecosystem – a community of living things and their environment

Adult pandas have few natural predators thanks to their large size and powerful build. However, snow leopards and large jackals may occasionally pose a threat, particularly to cubs or sick individuals. Panda cubs are especially vulnerable in their first few months of life when they are small and helpless.

Despite their peaceful nature, adult pandas are well-equipped to defend themselves when necessary. They have powerful jaws and strong muscles developed for crushing bamboo, which can also be used for self-defense. Their large size—comparable to that of American black bears—helps deter most potential predators. When threatened, pandas can also climb trees to escape danger, though they're not as agile as other bear species.

Historically, pandas may have had more natural predators, but as their range has contracted to remote mountain areas and their numbers decreased, encounters with large predators have become increasingly rare. This makes the preservation of their remaining habitat even more crucial for their continued survival.

---

predators – animals that hunt other animals for food

While pandas have few natural predators today, they face several serious threats, mostly from human activities affecting their forest home.

- **Habitat Fragmentation:** One of the biggest problems is that panda habitat has become fragmented—split into separate "islands" of forest. Imagine if your neighborhood was suddenly divided by huge highways, making it impossible to reach the grocery store. That's what happens to pandas when new roads and buildings cut through their forest home. This makes it hard for them to find mates or reach new areas when they need to.

- **Bamboo Boom-and-Bust:** Another challenge involves bamboo's unusual life cycle. Every few decades, entire bamboo forests flower and die at the same time. When this happens, pandas must travel to find different bamboo species to eat. But with their habitat divided into separate pieces, many pandas can't make these crucial journeys.

- **Climate Change:** As temperatures rise, scientists predict that up to 35% of panda habitat could become unsuitable for bamboo growth in coming decades. This could force pandas to move higher up mountains to find the cool, wet conditions they need.

- **Population Size:** The small number of pandas remaining in the wild creates additional challenges. With so few pandas left, it's harder for the species to maintain genetic diversity, which helps them stay healthy and adapt to changes in their environment.

Despite these challenges, panda conservation has seen amazing success. Thanks to China's efforts to protect panda habitat and ban logging in their forests, the wild panda population has grown from around 1,000 in the 1980s to nearly 1,800 today. Special breeding programs have also helped, and some pandas born in zoos have been successfully released into the wild.

In the wild, pandas typically live 14 to 20 years—about as long as a family dog. However, it's tricky for scientists to know exactly how long wild pandas live because studying them in their remote mountain forests can be challenging. These bears are experts at staying hidden!

When pandas live in zoos and breeding centers, where they receive regular checkups from veterinarians and plenty of fresh bamboo, they often live much longer—into their mid-20s or even early 30s. The oldest panda ever recorded was a female named Jia Jia, who lived to be 38 years old at Ocean Park in Hong Kong.

Thanks to decades of hard work protecting pandas, their numbers have grown significantly. In fact, pandas have made such a strong comeback that in 2016, scientists changed their status from "Endangered" to "Vulnerable"—a sign that these bears are doing much better.

In addition to wild pandas, another 600 pandas live in zoos and breeding centers around the world. These pandas are like safety nets for the species—they help scientists learn more about how pandas live, grow, and raise their cubs. Some pandas born in these centers have even been successfully released into the wild, where they've adapted well to life in the mountains.

Scientists work hard to keep track of how pandas are doing. They use methods like counting panda droppings, setting up special cameras that snap photos when pandas walk by, and carefully studying panda habitats. This careful monitoring helps make sure pandas continue to thrive.

Throughout this book, we've discovered what makes pandas one of nature's most extraordinary creatures. From their specialized "thumb" for handling bamboo to their remarkable recovery from near extinction, pandas show us just how amazing wildlife can be.

Pandas are full of surprises. Though they look like cuddly animals, they're actually powerful bears that can crush thick stalks with their strong jaws and swim across mountain streams. They've developed incredible ways to survive on a diet that would be impossible for most other animals. And despite being solitary animals, they've created complex ways of communicating with each other through sounds and scents.

These remarkable bears also teach us an important lesson about protecting nature. When people work together to save one species, they end up protecting entire mountain ecosystems. The forests where pandas live help keep mountain soils healthy and provide clean water for millions of people. By saving pandas, we also protect homes for countless other fascinating creatures, from golden monkeys to colorful pheasants.

Today, thanks to decades of hard work by scientists and conservationists around the world, more pandas live in the wild than at any time in the past 40 years. While they still face challenges, their recovery shows us that when people care enough about protecting nature, amazing things can happen.

As we look to the future, pandas remind us that every species is worth protecting. Through their gentle nature, surprising abilities, and remarkable comeback story, they've shown us that nature is full of wonders waiting to be discovered and preserved for future generations to enjoy.

Word Search

```
O O L R I M S M V U Y T O A Y Q
T O T K V A E E O H A B I T A T
A H D W D S A T C B Y C J Q S J
O D H N D L N S A Z A Z T V M J
N Q A J E A I Y L B M M V F E L
O P B P X M H S I C O H B G P C
I I T X T M C O Z D O L A O F F
T Z U I E A X C A J O L I L O A
A A Z W R M T E T Y F R V S W L
V V B V I O P I I U Z Z M Y M S
R N O I T C U D O R P E R I S E
E C M D Y I W M N N S Z I T Y T
S Q D H D X A T S W S L M R Q H
N L B R A C B N B T R H O X Z U
O D C O M M U N I C A T I O N M
C Z Q S B U C T N Y I T I W U B
O M N I V O R E S R F Q Q G F A
V V G H C C U O R P W A P A F C
B E A R S K X E Y R A T I L O S
A T L A C X T S N I A T N U O M
```

Adaptations	Cubs	Mountains
Bamboo	Dexterity	Omnivores
Bears	Ecosystem	Pandas
Camouflage	False Thumb	Reproduction
China	Habitat	Solitary
Communication	Mammals	Territory
Conservation	Metabolism	Vocalizations

INDEX

activity level, 18
appearance, 5, 6
bamboo, 5, 9, 13, 17, 18, 25, 29
bears, 5
breeding, 14, 21
camouflage, 6
China, 5, 29
climate change, 29
communication, 14, 17, 21
conservation, 29, 30, 33
cubs, 14, 17, 21, 22, 26
delayed implantation, 21
diet, 5, 9, 13, 18
digestive system, 9
ecosystem, 25
energy conservation, 13, 18
false thumb, 6, 10
food sources, 5, 9
forelimbs, 10
fur, 6, 10
grooming, 18
habitat, 6, 13, 25
habitat fragmentation, 29
jaws, 9, 10
lifespan, 30
mammals, 5
mating, 14, 21

metabolism, 10
migration, 17
movement, 13
nutrition, 9, 13
omnivores, 9
parenting, 14, 22
physical adaptations, 6, 9, 10
population, 29
predators, 26
pregnancy, 21
reproduction, 21, 22
senses, 10, 17
size, 6, 26
skulls, 9, 10
sleep, 18
smell, sense of, 10, 17
social structure, 14
swimming, 13
teeth, 9, 10
territory, 5, 17
threats, 26, 29
umbrella species, 25
Ursidae family, 5
vocalizations, 14, 21
water, 9, 13, 25
weight, 6
zoos, 29, 30

Published by Dylanna Press an imprint of Dylanna Publishing, Inc.
Copyright © 2025 by Dylanna Press
Author: Tyler Grady
All rights reserved. No part of this publication may be reproduced, stored in a retrieval system, or transmitted by any means, including electronic, mechanical, photocopying, or otherwise, without prior written permission of the publisher.

Although the publisher has taken all reasonable care in the preparation of this book, we make no warranty about the accuracy or completeness of its content and, to the maximum extent permitted, disclaim all liability arising from its use.

Printed in the U.S.A.

www.ingramcontent.com/pod-product-compliance
Lightning Source LLC
Chambersburg PA
CBHW040225040426
42333CB00051B/3449